VIRGINS

JESSE DARLING

Dedicated to Taki, who doesn't need it.

FOR SARAH, AFTER FIVE YEARS

Dear Military Wife,
I went alone & drunk to midnight mass
on a street rotten w gift shops & bridal boutiques. Thought of you,
& of what you call poetry. Thought of your kid & you know how I worry.
The headstones in chorus: much, most, moon & stars,
lies here, love always, devoted, dear, devoted etc.
In the church clustered haloes swarm round Jesus like white blood cells,
open eaves wide as spread legs above it.

Most of the theory exhausts me for real,
like it's bad drugs, bad medicine,
a noxious substance held at arm's length by clever people
who don't see the trouble, & how
it clouds the world & clogs the throat. Precocious misfits
from no-count shit towns forge a lonely bohemia through sheer force of will
& the fuelling cruelty of others. It isn't courage,
it's damage. In your skirt & dicksucking girlhood
you were the best & bravest of all the daisies in the field.

I don't want to talk about all that. I'm never going back.
1 shoe [unheeled], bag of sugar unspoiled, waste merch, no leaves,
mercy on the xmas lights, round cupped hole in the body unseen the crucible
of language itself & all the metaphors have fingers
& what we can't know we don't know. You know?

I dreamed I attended your wedding party —
there was wet confetti on the steps of the church & the moon
hung in its cradle like a skinny white baby in the crook of an arm.
Typed half of my immune system out into a chat window
& called it a love story. Red bricks, grey skies, girls out late in gooseflesh
& going straight, if that's what you call it,
was like being loamed in a box underground.

THE LOST ART OF LEISURE
An elegy for Bronwyn Pandemonium

The old Leisure Centre's a ruined church,
ancient architecture of ritual & obedience.
Holy rotten melamine marbled in bruisetone,
& the blue pool-hole gutted like a belly wound.
Blown like flies through fanged holes in the broken roof,
wet blossoms seed to maggot on the tile.
You hold the camera, & I turn around.
I raise my bottle, face you —
Fifteen years
& when you died I fought inside my working week
for five good minutes to mourn you right
but couldn't make the time. & so you came to find me,
between the idle hours of twelve to four at night.

You chewed at me for weeks. I took the whole day off.
The afternoon lay out long & cold without a claim
as you lay three long months in some big Berlin morgue
before your last old friends turned up your given name.

I cycled to the river & I bought us both a beer.
The Thames was stinking bloated & the clouds were thin.
I drank mine down from tab to cylinder, felt the sickly swim
& with my teeth I opened yours & poured the whole thing in.

As drug pig kids, we dreamed a life
where days were full, discrete & whole
like apples on a tree, & not this limping mulch
of weeks & months where hours dripped off the clock
like tears or spit. We take our shots & dip.

Funny but it's not,
how the pictures show us indistinct as ghosts,
like some kind of augur, although the light was bad
& we were almost drunk — our breath like hyacinth
& Listerine, the taste of a stomach eating itself.
At the all-day bar a booze rose blooms in every face.
We pour it up. We grin with all our skull.

SPEED, MACHINERY, VIOLENCE, YOUTH & INDUSTRY

Only a jobless kid living at his parents' place
would extol the virtues of labour and industry;
CrimethinC machos from lovely homes
in WASPy towns deride the worker drone.

Girlies can't keep up with these
excellent machines:
women & the mothers
motion sick from all the mones.

Marinetti dreamed of fuckbots, thought
death lay ass-up in the ditch. No homo
economicus, but death like anybody
was he / him, a bro down bad & vanquished
like any subby bitch.

        (Oedipussy yearns for Überkind
        to return & suck her tits.)

                        But the workers know
                & the mothers know
        & the real girls know
that industry is overrated.

To feint & sleight, to fake it —
        now that's the *real* art.

Marinetti carked it when his heart gave out,
like any other ancient fart.

CIRCUITS

The fair smells like pork grease & donuts, neons
bright in the rain. A drunk I went to school with
rides the ghost train alone. I go in my pocket for coins
& there's the lucky stone been weighing down my coat;
don't know who gave it me or why, but it's heavy
as any other blessing. Today they took so much blood,
a long list of tests to discover how good I could be
at giving or having life, & on the list it clearly said:
NOT DECEASED. Do u have everything u need she goes,
sex? Coffee? I'm like, *if u got it?* A large look passed between us
                    & then. I told her of the glory
of dreaming aloud & the long moments, sometimes days,
before it becomes terrifying. Wild flight, communion — & meanwhile
in here it's all awkward smiles & half entendres, as sickly
but bright-eyed I take my inevitable leave.

A ouija boredom puppets up the old ghost machinery
until it's all whirring out there in the were-world,
murmuring & yammering hum.
& the ghosts sing *whooooo,*
                    weeeeeeeeee,
                              ussssssssss!? !   ?

          & the punchline clicks!
          into!
          place!   !   !

USUAL CAVEATS

Becoming bourgeois wasn't about having or spending money,
going straight, clean clothes, whole foods. It took years to lose
the muscle memory of the laden tray; hen party, office drinks,
a bad boy's 35th. His friends click their fingers at you, touch your ass —
their eyes & foreheads shiny with cocaine. Oh benediction,
what a smashed bottle could / carve the wretched rind
of laughing mouth. But no.

In the open kitchen the cooks are eloquent accessory:
furnishing, prop, like moving parts. You see them
but you don't see them: sweated bandanas, reddened palms,
up on their feet for hours. Lungs, livers, hearts.

You know the stink of walk-in fridge,
meez-on-plass, blue roll, grey water —
but there you are, some long years later.
Two tables pushed together to launch an open glossy;
some young woman's money, wine. The corrosive flattery
that shames each time it speaks your name aloud.

A toast! To those for whom you have at best a soft contempt:
chin-chin! Pull back your teeth & skin.

I knew girls who studied art, made latte hearts for cash.
If you like a man who swipes your tips & slaps your assets
while you labour for his profit, you'll love marriage & children.
Oh they were proud, subjugated, & without rancor, though often tired
& though it is great to be good, it's better to live your only life aloud.

On the other side of prison, unemployment, asyla —
there's a fire. We stand around it. We raise our glasses.

VIRGINS

They say we aren't built for it. This species or another.
Crewcut & fatigued, a swollen head on the box says thin-lipped,
When most people talk about killing,
they are like virgins talking about sex.

A gathered clump of persons, dogs, children,
& their several prosthetics & familiars
with no cock in the fight & all the skin in the game
sit round a borrowed flatscreen on beer crates
to watch it all go down. Holy hero sado maso
kingdom glory shit, you know —

& here we go:

I'm drinking in my overcoat
when the Little Guy comes through.
Stiff legged hatchet faced florid
in suit jack & jeans, two fisting
cig & tin for the tough slit
of a stiff gob. *Don't shut yer hole.*
We eye each other haughtily,
2 bantams clucking in the pen.

Proud, mad, wounded, whatever:
we'll smack down the hand that scatters crumbs in the gutter,
& won't say thanks for dinner.
Pride is made despite; the likes of you & you & you & you
can't imagine what it's like.

They'll say it's counterrevolutionary,
but give me milk & mones & money,
whatever can be counted must be loved —
& give me the details of sex in the morning,
life enduring. Let impasse at long last be boring.

Very democratic is the failure of the body,
very democratic is the wait at A&E.
Deskilling as human & pledging secession,
singing shut me up & hold me tight.

We're waiting down the depot at midnight,
While the uniformed soldiers ignore us.

6 SHORT STORIES

1

My dream was a novel about death in which the hospital was a rich heterotopia hung with tapestries & signs: a seminar on how to address the dead as a demographic when writing or presenting. You gave me the wings of 4 black geese in a plastic bag lined with newspaper. *Collateral*, you said with a nod, & you were gone.

2

In the dream I woke up poisoned vomiting spattered with blood. *I'm feeling good*, you said. It was your only birthday. I was having a sex thing with a dead girl but we were in two different places. Jammed my mobility cane into the o-ring of a strapon harness & went lurching into the broken gait like the old one-two.

3

The boys I loved in childhood were saltwater corpses floppy stacked on a floating bier & rotting in the sun. Each summer another on the pile. Out of an ice-blue sky I landed my plane on the water. I took off my man's flying suit. I took off my woman's body. I dived & disappeared.

4
We swam in the flooded church, far below us dark rusted crosses & the barnacled altar, organ & pulpit blowing quiet bubbles at the bottom. As they were hiding the body in the slop house they discovered that he had breasts & a vagina but dead is dead anyway, amen & rest his soul.

5
Drawn under duress a crowded folio of blueprints became a choir of buildings, each one shot through the mortise with pain. Long fields rushing past the windows in slow motion capture of a landscape experiencing orgasm. *What really happened behind that wall, Jesse?* Tears because truthfully I don't know, I mean I think I don't know —

6
We thought it was terrorism but it was just advertising. Holy violence of the open-fisted filigree as it met my upturned face on its way to ground. I stuck my finger into the hole in the middle & lifted the skirt on the lid of the world, eyes rolling back all the way to sky.

ARMINIUSSTRASSE 5 O'CLOCK

Gut-brain rides again, with its mucus & ectoplasm:
subconscious is the shit that stops up your sight. A bright hole
like a caved-in mine with the world's undigested backlog
of prolapsed sorrow, & this stuff goes back & back
a couple hundred years. Bad habits of the ancestors,
violence, resentment, paucity of culture, hole in the middle
of modernity; sounds clever but feels stupid & brutal, like whatever
else is visited on the body & the ground in the name of What Must Be,
& life is equally cheap & dear wherever you go:
old boys in the square, a daddy with a baby on his chest,
someone resting on a bench with crutches aside like two long palms,
kids out chalking in the sun. How fragile a thing is peace
& how contingent. A heady dereliction comes settling in,
sugary permissions of the first of many drinks,
a floral ejaculate plugging every sudden hole in my head.

Well, I broke my own rule & I had one or two,
trying always to break through the roof of my own mouth
into the splayed sinew & the swaying stem. Pollinator, medulla,
let it come. I spread my hands out on the street:
between my fingers, only open ground. & this ground,
it is wordless, wordless.

NO FLAGS NO HASHTAGS

It's all ritual theatre until somebody gets buried alive in the basement wrapped in packing blankets: I wasn't sorry because he used to ring the bell all night & once scared the girls by asking politely if we'd mind him nailing himself to my crucifix. There's the whole #YesAllWomen thing & then there's actual commerce & there's physical violence & there are women who, for whatever reason, are not. One of the girls disappeared that night. We trace her last movements on the mourning cam. Where did she go when she left the dryout depot? With my eye I wanted to go there, to the end of that road. With my whole body I wanted to go there

LISTEN UP LADIES

They weren't the best minds of your generation ok,
most of 'em were rich kids with addictions
& unprocessed trauma, same as the "best minds" of my generation.
Like all my friends are Other & they're p much all Significant ok,
like glory in the highest, exempt from sale, use, denigration in culture,
degradation of the word or flesh, deconstruction by critical theorists et al.

Everyone's talking about new year, new york and new meat now!!
Lethal flooding predicted just about everywhere
but we're all kinda flaking on making a plan??!
We're awful!! Lili Marlene as pixel death,
cumsplashes on a flatscreen, green M&M's as racial diversity
& how far would YOU go
to maintain your, like,
wounded otherness!???

O libido, o wunschmaschine, o Mary Poppins!!
Is it OPPRESSION or is it just *inconvenience*?
Business as usual in the suffering farms, but be a good girl
& don't be racist ok? Pass the prosecco
& watch mummy get fabulous!! Like cry me a river,
hire me a sweatshop,
& put it on a t shirt so I know it's like, *real*

HIGH AROUSAL 2

In my dream 2 small children in red Adidas tracksuits were adamant that they were dressed in costume as streaky bacon. Some painter bro added me on Instagram then I went back to sleep & dreamed that his dick was a pod at the end of a long skin tassle, soft as lips & dripping with the milk he dipped in, like a cutlet waiting for panko. Meanwhile out between the middle-aged straights who don't need words for what they are & the middle class kids who could read you the latest manual, our glitter just gets stuck in the wrinkles, starts looking like a crusted scab. She couldn't get hard except for the stirred semi she called a pacino stub & *desire never made flesh is chastity*, she said: *it's a question of intentional branding*. Our toothbrushes lounged at drunken angles in their mouldy cup like the last stragglers at a hot tub party. 73 minutes past the hour.

ONLY FOOLS AND HORSES GET THE BLUES

Here I am: the skelly in your closet,
doubled over, ratineed,
limp-wristed at the bended knee,
& camp as a folding bed.
It's broken but it works

& if jesus was a carpenter
then God's a bodger, a bugger
with his allen key that fits & twists
in every greasy hole. I *LOVE* him,
& I love you. Fingers are clumsy
when erect, but teeth are very fine.

We walked the streets
with all our colours blazing,
trooping the forbidden flag
& lagging in the march.
Like every time they came in flying
to smash up skulls & kneecaps
& trampled our little party favours
just to show us who's DEMOCRACY.

It doesn't make you stronger,
just chews away all winter.
The union were on the phone,
say there's nothing they can do. But you —

crosswise & starfished,
you're tenting your raiment
with nipples stiff & grin
as bare as bone.

O my love,
nothing in this greasy life
is half as hard
as my big dick
& your thick head.

AFTER ST AGNES

Why don't you just hit me if you hate me so much
I asked you, I pleaded. It wasn't a sex thing,
my violence was frightening. I was bawling on the fire escape
& your mother was calling the police on me
because in her book, blistered
& parched as it was from repetitive fingering,
the hole through which jesus got away
should be shuttered inside
FOREVER, or else PUNISHED

for opening opening wide, the great tide
rising in my spittle gland
& loosing its ancient muscle
into the wet white throat
of the restaurant toilet
like *thank you, thank you*.

O god was there in me, the finger in my gullet
pointing toward the light.

I tell you what, let's us play Eden.
I'll be the snake or I can be Adam.
You can be Eve. No —
you be the garden.

HIGH AROUSAL

Unlimited pay-per-view in a hotel etc,
& when you took your clothes off I wasnt menna be looking at u
nor you at me, but I noticed your flesh
shaped by them long years you been walking the way you do.

Blue bleach & piss yellow mix in the bathtub's wet gusset
forming a perfect soft gradient in a palette of Tumblrtones:
doing this way by beamer light visualisation
& an open wound going *YES*.

My body confused by the data
wondered if this was erotic or traumatic.
All the way home in the taxi I sat there alive.
They wrote my name on a Starbucks
& I liked the way they spelled it,
made me feel different like possible,
& you were only 'going home'.

A girl's huge beautiful ass in stretch blue satin,
fake yew lions at the Savoy,
Waterloo Bridge lit up like a shit wet Vegas.

Nobody ever smelled as good as this random big guy on the tube
with womanish thighs in webdev blue jeans:
tears in my eyes for I wanna be near it.

My whole life's girl writes to say
that her youngest is so much like me that I might be the father.
Point is, I no longer care about being beautiful.
Wish you didn't either. Yours regretfully,

IN MEDIAS RES

In the middle of this the course of our life, I stopped
& everybody got out of their car.
The crickets roared. Wind farm sliced up blue in chorus,
like syncopated swimmers, all muscle blade & grace.
Young biker soft-shouldered with his leathers off. No ass to speak of.
& not much of a face. He whispered of the car on fire ahead,
all reverent, & pointed, said: *just up there*. & so it was.

I walk the broken line like I once walked in the bar,
bang down the middle, toes out, & I flashed my brights
at all the girls & boys. Kids, I was gorgeous,
I mean drop dead, & I knew it too;
it was all I knew, & not much else. But I was full of speed,
& driven by longing for my life, for fire,
or a ride out of town. & I still thought, back then,
that people staring meant desire.

Years pass. & when at last I let the bleach grow out,
I see that my hair has turned grey. An hour or two goes by.
Frosted tips in the camper van tut tuts on the shoulder.
Parched mouth poppies tongue the verge.
Quiet of afternoon except for the rumours, the distant siren,
& breathing gentle fire ahead, the empty car.

When we all drove past
in single file, we marvelled as it burned.
What damage. What elegance. *What happened?*
What happened here?

TO HELL WITH ALL THAT

John Wayne and I gone strange and stupid in the rerun,
cadavers cantering on the endless spool and the script like simple math.

In a post-patriarchal mainstream, a hippy cis divorcee
twice married into the officer class before the great defunding,
is celebrated for her bestselling title
Delicious Sorrow: Mourning Male Supremacy.

You get wasted and rave about the Property and Lifestyle feature
in which identical white girls in scented pantyliners
show your avatar around a series of magical showhomes,
boasting big blue windows and jaw-wide doorways,
all lubricated with light like a hole in the head.

Bore me like one of your straight girls, I said.

Big Hollywood a bloated gut metabolising America,
and if only if only those zombies sought revenge,

it would be wounded knee all over again,
and every cowboy would find his place
where he existed a mere moment between
the Enclosures Act and the end of mining

and as for the eternal ingenue, I wanted to be inside her,
but tired of her euphemisms because death is the basic integer.

No daisies without the grave, I said, but she was pressing flowers into books.
The flowers were bright, wet, full of tongues and stamina.

They'll stain, I said.

It'll fade, she said.

Like everything, I said.

But the ingenue was illuminated
by her own pale fire.

The bluebeard Hitchcock said blondes make the best victims,
and that's what they mean by having more fun.
The white girls wear their throats open in spring, coquettish.

Some things are aeternal,
she said, and curtsied,
springs creaking all the way down.

MARCH OF THE VALEDICTORIANS

You introduced yourself with the affect of a rich kid: belligerently charming and on the level. I swaggered, I staggered. With my epithets and defences I was undeferential but terrified, rich in debts, epithets, and the currency of disease. My poverty was a tender in which you keenly wished to invest.

You had your portfolio; I had my scribbled towels under the bed, a little scar tissue. It was the raw material, the real thing.

So this is me, I said; I'd point to something and make a clumsy equivalence. *Same!* you'd squeal. Your high five clipped the side of my face.

When you demanded that the world respect your pronouns it was glorious. Alone in my bedroom I cheered for you. I became your big brother, by which I mean your mother. *I don't* feel like a mother, I said. The doctor ignored me and kept writing in my file before reaching between my legs and twisting his thingie around. I cooked a big stew for your friends and they pretended to admire my decor while screening calls from their parents in the suburbs, who pay the rent at the revolutionary commune. When I said something unfunny and your colleague said *girl, I know!*, I'll admit I felt gratified. A million trust fund art school projects about the Freudian homosexual and one's own bad lot.

IN WHICH 'COLOUR IS FREED FROM OBJECTIVE CONTEXT AND BECOMES THE SUBJECT IN ITSELF'

Colour Field was the punchline
of a bitter joke. Was cartography,
superstructure. It was plain
and territory, partitioned like country,
canvas wide as army barracks.

My kid could do that,
and this is how they pinked the map:
with ferrous one-eyed vision machines
down whose noses the explosion of the possible
was a boundlessness left empty by god:

The gun:
ONE.
The camera:
oh.

Now watch as it surfaces out. Covered over.
and everything blends into nothing, or something,
and the violence is that

    'the dialectic'

does not even begin to articulate
what was lost in amongst / in between
enchantment / conquest / & terrain.

You knew to recognise the museum
as the big house, charnel house.
Mausoleum. The manor.
Yeah, but you can go there.
Yeah, but you don't.

THE MUSTER

A whole life long the bastards girled me blue.
They girled me in the sick house,
they girled me in the wedding room,
they girled me in a plastic bag down by the tracks.

I stepped over the thing in the sack that was me
& went to Stansted Airport on the express train.
I was in amongst a clutch of Hens, hustled up chubby
& armed to the teeth with wheelie bags & cock whistles,
tan line epaulettes, each tired head tiara'd like the cross of courage,
the grimmest of grunt packs back from the flak.
We went bruising down the line, ensemble,
& clouds gathered like tumours on the flat,
great whorled bosoms grey with milk.

They can take & take it from you,
until you'll beg to sign it over. No metaphor
but war for all, wall-to-wall & in the air,
when suddenly the light broke through
in military blue.

The ceiling on the sick house,
above the wedding room (so lovely!)
the ceiling on the world above the tracks.

& the girled belong to everyone,
so we filed & filed along.
Kind old birds with booze breath
touched me up & buoyed me on.

Buoyed me & they buoyed me.
They held me up amongst them.
Conduits of an older wisdom,
they saw it & they knew.

Uniform, the wall to sky,
the surging, virgin blue.

ANALEMMA

There is a special kind of boredom in small towns & shit jobs
that builds up & up until it blows. Libidinal. Old men round here
will go to their graves before taking a hint: manic pixie dream bag lady,
neurodiversity in an ageing population,
the spirit of the megamart, cast loose of lithe kawaii.

In the end I outgrew everything,
& then in revenge it outgrew me.

It Gets Better™,
which only means you learn to trust the claws & teeth
by which you stay alive.
New prophets maraud the cloud like repent or pay here,
cleanse thine heart, sign up, be saved.

I sat alone on the warm stone of a monument to recent empire
& watched the river while flies died in the floodlights. Beer #1
like treacle from the can, & 1 dead pixel on the billboard
like a missing tooth. They used to keep the liquor
by the altar. Sunset filter, wide lens above,
surround, a parallax, relief. *Who's scared?*
said a mother to her child, & I overheard.
Is dolly scared? Is monster scared?
Is MUMMY scared?
Yes, said the baby.
No! said the mother, *Mummy's not scared!*
Liar, I thought. *Liar*

DEVANT LEZ ENFANTS

On a rubber-tiled technicolour tundra,
zoo-born beasts with Christianised names
play out their petit psychodramas
in a post-race animalia of Boys, Girls
& occasionally someone else, complete
with own storyline, dialectically suffering
& thriving etc, loved & affirmed by
both parents & indeed the industry itself.

Dinosaurs, carnivores & walking pork
smiling in police hats & princess dresses
drive happy cars through happy lands.
No arrests are made, nor laws upheld
beyond the bright white birthright
of the endless happy ending
of the oozing Marxist model
in whichever ever after
(*cue canned children's laughter*).

We clean our fangs with fluoride,
pull socks on over claws, wash paws,
change clothes, & remember!
We NEVER say yes to the stranger.

Sugar, cotton, polyethylene,
good breast of the free market,
a buy-in, a lullaby. Scream
of the siren. How To Talk
To Your Children About
People Who Want You
To Talk To Your Children,
about Santa Claus, sanity, manifest
destiny, gender & dying & debt,

as puff-hats & glory dogs
are pinkly put to worthy earthwork

on the soft edge of a hard machine
guzzling blood & fossil grease.
Bent backs, deferred grief,
counted heads, cold shoulders,
muddied knees (*knees & toes*)

& eyes & ears & mouth, God knows
How To Talk To Your Children
about the children at the border,
about the bodies in the desert,
about the big red motor-car
at the end of the world, smiling
death with his panda eyes,
pandemic, fairy princess,
jumping frog & wind-up mouse.
Brother cockroach, chubby maggot,
talking mouth of open wound
& wind-up gun & broken house.

Gunshots for Tinkerbell!
Land mines for Tinkerbell!
Wherever you are —
if you *really believe —*

It erodes & corrodes
& explodes as it goes

enfin, at issue:
we *all*
        fall
            down.

HOTEL-WAS-WIT

Remember when we found a Henry Miller book in a pile of dust at the bottom of a box full of hand drawn kiddy porn on the first day in the squatted hotel? We rode our beer buzz through the afternoon and took turns to read out loud, and we laughed at this randy old man, like any wash-up at the bar tryna get his end off for a drink or two. So this was literature! How the grand old men all flopped their dicks out across the page like applause at the opera, like a round of safari gunfire in those pale colonial bollock-shorts, a flam paradiddle of back slaps in chorus. And how they canonised each other's fantasies, reverent as a mouth around a cock. True we were cruel in youth but this was cruelty as literature and cruelty as culture and cruelty as the only sex anyone had ever sanctioned for the likes of us, lambs in the door jamb tryna pose for the slaughter in the best of our bloodiness — being as how we were nothing but a bunch of perambulating holes on legs, barely holding in what would surely always out. When someone cut up a bit of speed left over from the night before it was cosy and sweet, a gesture to keep the moment going a bit longer so we'd all be together there until night fell, knees crowded tight and beers winking open like shy holes and the soft fibrous electricity between mouth and beer and hole and eye starting to flow a little faster in sequence and pulse.

SETTLING

First, cop to the extractive logic of producing cultural objects
(poems, sculptures) from the raw material of experience;
the mining wound cuts deep & jagged; each word a plumb,
a claim. Ancestral silt exhumed & put to still, the dead unsettled loam.

The hubris of the living. My mother nearly died but somehow lived,
& I — against my better judgement — wrote it down. Silence
is death & golden, death banned outright, & nothing gold can stay.
What's left inside? The sempiternal: chew toy, padding, plastic bag,
wrapper, naphtha, grandmama. We keep moving up & on.

I went to the oak with my mushrooms & libations,
& there among the garbage I got down damp on bended knee
I said *sorry, I'm so sorry,*
& with my little affects made a circle round the tree,
avoiding human turd & broken glass, ashamed of all my kin.

& then the message hit, my word —
Mycelia! I laughed aloud;
no atoning for the gift of shit:
may sacred waste at suckling root remain interred.

THE WORK

I woke, drank coffee, read the news,
bundled up the kiddo & we made it
out the door. A jangling choir of little woes:
spilt milk, a band-aid, meds —
the morning passed in 12-step prayers
sent through by willing friends.

Pale skin-toned prayer hands, heart eyes face,
heart heart crystal ball. The psychic on the podcast said:
you've got to do the work.

I phoned a friend & cried at last
— for her, for me, for all of us —
the labour nearly killed them both,
the doctors don't get paid enough,
they saved a life, but fucked her up.
Still, now they're getting by.

The baby's doing well. *Just us*, I joked,
said *you'll be fine*. Which was not a lie.

Stayed home as asked & read the doctrine
in a bathtub warmed by urine. Kids, you know,
the skid marks, gusts & suds & throes,
the feral hole where life abides. We try
to get along. & when I heard
they'd banned the work —
online and off, in schools —
I knew that it was really starting now,
or else, that it was done.

A lucky sense of loss
for all those nights spent arguing the toss
at tables in the squats & bars, & old Karl Marx,
& what he thought would come to pass,

so cute & quaint & faraway. & now
abundance forecast — at long last —
the astro-grifters cheer us on
to throw it down for house & home
on something nice — "indulgent" —
that costs a weekly wage.

But fuck it, *dear ones*,
burn that sage. It's payday now,
or so they say; & anyway,
just what else is there?

Something bloomed;
we're dancing in the kitchen
like we did on nine-one-one.
R-E-S-P-E-C-T! Me & the little one,
we whooped & threw ourselves around the room.

I got too drunk & read the cards,
promiscuous, incendiary —
these days of heady luxury;
the year we wished would end.

We'll look back on these as good times.
Yours always, love you. *Send*.

DREAM POEM FOR LUX

In the dark a little shape looms familiar on the brink,
arms all laden with friends. Steps practiced but heavy
over the barrier. I reach up to catch the fall, as always,
& roll into awkward embrace. Light rises on a spiked sleep,
sentience in the drift, like water dreaming itself,
& all these fish! Elegant mackerel & sharks on the ritz
in pearls & silk, every living thing a haul
in the storming Spirit of the new New World.
Who needs 'em, these beds & gulches?
Fish are for eating & life is for living, no less
murderous for all we think we know.

As a wet red dress I stood floundering in a hotel,
Somehow left alone with the men, & then alone again.
Mug's game. Left that bitch behind like beauty,
stretched out the fishy beast in the snouted bag of me:
my bedshirt damp dry, wet rope, warm rubber.
Alive or dead now only homing to another.

Oh my little carbon footprint, may she live to turn it over,
land up something much better than I gave her.

Without the commitment, conversation, controversial edits and combined genius of Chris, Claire, Lauren, Liana and Shayna of the Anarchist Poetry Crit Collective, most of these poems would not exist. Thank you for being part of the experimental love work, out beyond whichever institution somewhere. Thanks also to Elaine Kahn, whose Poetry Field School began it all, and to LA Warman of the Warman School, whose pedagogies taught me a thing or two. Shouts to Jack and Azad for their writing and their chat, and to Imran Perretta, for all the talking and thinking we've done over the years. To Siddhartha and Erin of Hopscotch Reading Room; Patty, Rebecca, Elijah, Maru and Tracy of the a.p. poetry workshop in Berlin; friends and coleagues Hannah Gregory, Musa Okwonga, Roy Claire Potter, Lizzie Homersham, Season Butler, Sarah Harrison, Clay AD, Kameelah Janan Rasheed, Orion Facey, Megan Nolan, Caspar Heinemann, Miloš Trakilović, Emily Berry and Elene Abashidze, who have sometimes shown me ways to think about writing (and write about thinking), which remains a work in progress. Thanks to all the muses — who had better unionise — and to those named and unnamed friends, lovers, strangers and colleagues who show up here through no fault of their own.

'Only Fools and Horses Get The Blues' is after Claire Sosienski-Smith (following a provocation by Liana Mack), and in particular remixes a couple of lines from their poems 'An Emergency' and 'Cyborg Blues'.

Versions of these poems have appeared in *Granta, Tripwire, Blush, In The Current of the Situation* (Dolce Publications, 2021) *Altered States* (Ignota Press, 2021) and *There are new suns / bruised blossoms* (Kunstraum Niederoestereich, on the occasion of the exhibition 'Life constantly escapes', 2021). To the editors who saw something in these — and to you, for having read this far: thank you.

Published by Monitor Books
June 2023
ISBN 978-1-80352-273-9

Second edition

Dust jacket printed by Sonsoles Print Studio

Monitor Books Ltd.
Deptford, London

Designed by Chaosmos Studio

monitorbooks.co.uk

Jesse Darling is an artist and intermittent poet who (at the time of writing) is both living and working.

ISBN 978-1-80352-273-9